The Fairy Without Wings

Copyright ©2014 Nicola Gothard.
All rights reserved.

Published by Generation 2050

www.generation2050project.org

Aluna Lilova was a fairy from Pixie Meads, a magical land where the sun shone on the rainbow leaves.

She watched on by, as the other fairies flew up high, weaving their magic in the sky.

Aluna was a fairy without wings.

They told Aluna her wings would grow when she learned to follow her heart, but she did not know where to start.

So she took to her feet and travelled the lands across moonflower meadows and velvet sands, but still her heart would not speak.

Aluna looked up to the sky just as a shooting star passed by.

She decided to follow the star no matter how far.

Soon she stood at the edge of a deep dark wood.
Her heart started to beat, and although her legs wobbled she pushed on with her feet.

The forest was dark, but her heart sparked bright to light her path through the night.
As she peered through the trees, she quietly called out,
'I come in peace, don't hurt me please'.

To her surprise she suddenly saw two giant green eyes and big hairy paws, with razor sharp claws.

As her sight adjusted to the night, she began to see a blaze of fiery striped fur and then came out a little purr.

Aluna had never seen such a beast, he was three times her height – at least.

He looked so scared, caught and tangled in a thorny snare.

Aluna worried he was bleeding, hungry and needed feeding, so she hurried to release him.

She worked so hard she did not know her wings had begun to grow, up they came, as she worked through pain, in wind and rain, then snow.

Finally the beast was free but when he stood he fell to his knees.
So she gave him a hug and lots of love.

When she saw her wings for the first time, her heart began to sing and chime.
'Oh, I've been so blind, kindness is what I've been trying to find'.

The beast looked longingly at a door in the sky, then turned to Aluna to explain why...

'I fell through that flap in the sky, and I don't know how to get home,' he cried.

'It's ok, don't cry. I have my wings now, I can fly!'

And so up they soared to the door.

They pushed and pushed until in they whooshed, to another world, where giants milled preparing a feast. 'The cat is back,' they trilled, and all rushed over to greet the beast, as Aluna Lilova made a hasty retreat.

Aluna Lilova's journey was over, for she had found her wings and became the fairy that protects all living things.

Legend has it she can be seen in cat eyes but only as a shooting star passes by.

Generation 2050

Inspiring generations of compassionate world citizens one book at a time!

Generation 2050 is a non-profit children's book publisher. At Generation 2050 we believe in the power of story-telling to change the world for the better. We publish books which inspire and empower children to become responsible world citizens who act with compassion towards other people, animals and the planet. For more information on Generation 2050 and for other titles in the series please visit our website.

 generation2050project    @gen2050    GENERATION2050PROJECT

WWW.GENERATION2050PROJECT.ORG

www.ingramcontent.com/pod-product-compliance
Lightning Source LLC
Chambersburg PA
CBHW080520020526
44113CB00055B/2537